4th Grade English Workbook
Cursive Writing Perfection

BABY PROFESSOR
EDUCATION KIDS

Speedy Publishing LLC
40 E. Main St. #1156
Newark, DE 19711
www.speedypublishing.com

Copyright 2018

All Rights reserved. No part of this book may be reproduced or used in any way or form or by any means whether electronic or mechanical, this means that you cannot record or photocopy any material ideas or tips that are provided in this book.

Cursive Sentence Writing

Trace and rewrite the sentences.

Childhood is a short season.

Life is short.

Cursive Sentence Writing

Trace and rewrite the sentences.

You can do it. Everyone can do it.

Be patient and understanding.

Cursive Sentence Writing

Trace and rewrite the sentences.

In teaching others we teach ourselves.

Life is short, and it is here to be lived.

Cursive Sentence Writing

Trace and rewrite the sentences.

Good things, when short, are twice as good.

Practice makes perfect.

Cursive Sentence Writing

Trace and rewrite the sentences.

Light travels faster than sound.

The best things in life make you sweaty."

Cursive Sentence Writing

Trace and rewrite the sentences.

Life is the sum of all your choices.

In spite of the cost of living, it's still popular.

Cursive Sentence Writing

Trace and rewrite the sentences.

Life is simple, its just not easy.

The purpose of life is a life of purpose.

Cursive Sentence Writing

Trace and rewrite the sentences.

You Live Only Once.

You are your choices.

Cursive Sentence Writing

Trace and rewrite the sentences.

Whatever happens, take responsibility.

What's done is done.

Cursive Sentence Writing

Trace and rewrite the sentences.

Ultimately love is everything.

Too clever is dumb.

Cursive Sentence Writing

Trace and rewrite the sentences.

Thoughts rule the world.

Think outside the box.

Cursive Sentence Writing

Trace and rewrite the sentences.

Paint the town red.

Faith can move mountains.

Cursive Sentence Writing

Trace and rewrite the sentences.

Follow your own star.

God doesn't make junk.

Cursive Sentence Writing

Trace and rewrite the sentences.

What is normal anyway?

Happiness depends upon ourselves.

Cursive Sentence Writing

Trace and rewrite the sentences.

It's never too late.

Beginnings are always messy.

Cursive Sentence Writing

Trace and rewrite the sentences.

Yes, No, Maybe So.

Never doubt your instinct.

Cursive Sentence Writing

Trace and rewrite the sentences.

Work hard stay humble.

Courage doesn't always roar.

Cursive Sentence Writing

Trace and rewrite the sentences.

Tomorrow is another day.

Dance lightly with life.

Cursive Sentence Writing

Trace and rewrite the sentences.

Just go for it.

Ride like the wind.

Cursive Sentence Writing

Trace and rewrite the sentences.

Nobody cares about it.

Don't worry, be happy.

Cursive Sentence Writing

Trace and rewrite the sentences.

Think Less, Feel More.

Enjoy the little things.

Cursive Sentence Writing

Trace and rewrite the sentences.

Your Time is Now.

Success and nothing less.

Cursive Sentence Writing

Trace and rewrite the sentences.

No feeling is final.

We are what we think.

Cursive Sentence Writing

Trace and rewrite the sentences.

I think therefore I am.

All limitations are self imposed.

Cursive Sentence Writing

Trace and rewrite the sentences.

Imagination is greater than detail.

Don't sweat the small stuff.

Cursive Sentence Writing

Trace and rewrite the sentences.

Be gentle first with yourself.

Make each day your masterpiece.

Cursive Sentence Writing

Trace and rewrite the sentences.

Another Sunrise, Another New Beginning

Failure cannot cope with persistence.

Cursive Sentence Writing

Trace and rewrite the sentences.

Risk, care, dream and expect.

Big egos have little ears.

Cursive Sentence Writing

Trace and rewrite the sentences.

May you be happy always.

Make yourself necessary to somebody.

CPSIA information can be obtained
at www.ICGtesting.com
Printed in the USA
BVHW021143020723
666682BV00008BA/318

9 781682 601204